# The Creek

## The Past and Present of the Muscogee

by Danielle Smith-Llera

Consultant:
Brett Barker, PhD
Associate Professor of History
University of Wisconsin–Marathon County

**CAPSTONE PRESS**
a capstone imprint

Fact Finders Books are published by Capstone Press,
1710 Roe Crest Drive, North Mankato, Minnesota 56003
www.mycapstone.com

**Library of Congress Cataloging-in-Publication Data**
Names: Smith-Llera, Danielle, 1971- author.
Title: The Creek : the past and present of the Muscogee / by Danielle
  Smith-Llera.
Description: North Mankato, Minnesota : Capstone Press, 2016. | Series:
  Fact finders. American indian life | Includes bibliographical references
  and index. | Description based on print version record and CIP data
  provided by publisher; resource not viewed.
Summary: Explains Creek history and highlights Creek life in modern
  society.
Identifiers: LCCN 2015046717 (print) | LCCN 2015043528 (ebook) | ISBN
  978-1-5157-0238-2 (library binding) | ISBN 978-1-5157-0242-9 (pbk.) |
  ISBN 978-1-5157-0246-7 (ebook pdf)
Subjects: LCSH: Creek Indians—History—Juvenile literature. | Creek
  Indians—Social life and customs—Juvenile literature.
Classification: LCC E99.C9 (print) | LCC E99.C9 S65 2016 (ebook) | DDC
  975.004/97385—dc23
LC record available at http://lccn.loc.gov/2015046717

**Editorial Credits**
Alesha Halvorson, editor; Richard Korab, designer; Tracy Cummins and
Pam Mitsakos, media researchers; Tori Abraham, production specialist

**Photo Credits**
Capstone Press: 19; Corbis: 5 (bottom inset), 14-15; Getty Images: Kean
Collection, 13; Library of Congress: cover (top), 1; Native Stock Pictures:
Angel Wynn, cover, 22, 24, 28; North Wind Picture Archives: 4-5, 6-7, 10,
26; Shutterstock: Blulz60, 20, Boris15, 25, davemhuntphotography, 9, David
Fossler, 16, 29 (background), Everett Historical, 12, Jeffrey M. Frank, 21,
life_is_fantastic, 18, Marina Kurrle, cover (background); Wikimedia, 17

Printed and bound in China.
009464F16

# Table of Contents

# Seeds of the Ancestors

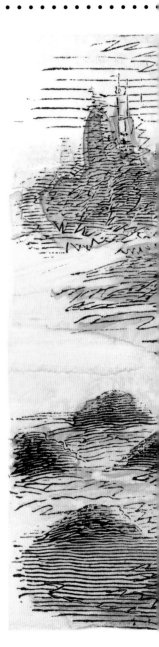

Tractors rumble through fields of the Muscogee Creek Nation. Farmers plow rows for squash, tomatoes, and peppers. Some farmers remember foods that nourished their ancestors for thousands of years. In their fields, vines twist around pumpkins. Large-kerneled corn, called safke, stands tall.

Whether they work with tractors, computers, or microscopes, Muscogee today feel connected to their ancestors. They work together to weave their history into daily life.

ancestor: family member who lived a long time ago

*The Creek planted a large-kerneled corn called safke.*

### National seal
The seal of the Muscogee Creek Nation hangs in the National Council Office in Okmulgee, Oklahoma. The plow and bundle of wheat in the center honor their long tradition of agriculture.

# Chapter 1

# Early Life

Rivers and streams flowing through present-day Georgia and Alabama connected a group of American Indian tribes hundreds of years ago. They built villages along the shores. Canoes turned the waterways into roads between communities. They called themselves the Mvskoke—the Muscogee. British later met them along these rivers and creeks and called them the Creek.

The Muscogee lived well. River flooding made garden soil rich with nutrients. Villages swelled with people. The Muscogee founded new towns. To stay strong the communities formed a **confederacy**. Residents of up to 500 towns made decisions together and protected each other.

Inside each Muscogee town, tribe members worked together. The chief made decisions with the help of a **council** of advisers and priests. They discussed a problem until everyone agreed on a solution.

*Muscogee communities worked together and helped each other.*

**confederacy:** union of people or groups with a common goal
**council:** group of people elected to make decisions for a larger group

## VILLAGE LIFE

Everyone in a Muscogee village worked to provide food and clothing for its people. Women worked in family gardens. With their hands and sharp sticks, they planted, weeded, and harvested beans, squash, corn, and sunflowers. Men worked side by side in farm fields that fed the entire village.

Women headed into the forest with handmade grass-woven baskets. They returned with wild rice, nuts, and berries. In pots shaped from river clay, they cooked stews over fires. Children worked alongside women when they were old enough.

Men helped fill cooking pots with meat and fish. They stunned fish with a poisonous plant and gathered the floating fish. They hunted deer, bear, turkey, and rabbits with traps and bows and arrows. Women wove grass and stitched deerskin into skirts and shirts for themselves and apronlike coverings for the men.

Members of the village also worked together to teach Muscogee children. Elders told stories about how the world began and about the history of the tribe. Uncles taught nephews how to hunt, and aunts taught nieces how to cook.

## CLANS

Muscogee were loyal to their families and also to their clans. Members of the same clan were *descendants* of the same female ancestors. Each Muscogee baby was born into its mother's clan.

Some clans, such as the Alligator Clan and the Sweet Potato Clan, were named after plants and animals that nourished the tribe. The Wind Clan was named after a powerful force of nature.

Members of the same clan did not always live in the same village. But they called each other "brother" and "sister" even when meeting for the first time. Some Muscogee today still have special relationships with clan members.

They might consider a person's clan when making friends, finding a business partner, or choosing a leader.

*Some clans were named after powerful animals, such as deer and wolves.*

Elders taught children to respect nature. They believed animals and plants had spirits. Corn was so **sacred** to the Muscogee that they held ceremonies while it ripened and while it was harvested. Tribe members danced and sang around a fire burning at the center of each village. It was a time for forgiveness and new beginnings.

**elder:** older person whose experience makes him or her a leader
**descendant:** person who comes from a particular group of ancestors
**sacred:** holy

9

Tomo-chichi, a Creek chief, offered furs for trade to British General James Oglethorpe in the colony of Georgia.

# ENGLISH ARRIVAL

The British settled the colony of Carolina in 1660. They began exploring the rivers in surrounding areas. The Muscogee they met in present-day Georgia were interested in trading native goods, such as deerskins, for English cloth, guns, and metal tools.

Trade with the British changed Muscogee daily life. Cloth gradually replaced deerskin clothing. Like the British, they hunted with rifles and farmed with plows. They built homes out of logs instead of cane and plaster. Meanwhile, Muscogee living farther away from British colonies, in present-day Alabama, continued living like their ancestors.

The British and their Muscogee allies also fought wars together. Together they pushed the French off their territories in the early 1700s. Later, in 1778, some Muscogee helped the British fight colonists who wanted to form their own country. But the British lost the American Revolution, and the Muscogee lost their powerful ally. Now they feared losing their tribal lands to the United States

ally: person, group, or country that helps and supports another

# Chapter 2

# Moving West

Life in the new nation was stressful for the Muscogee. The U.S. government built roads through native territory. Some American settlers attacked Muscogee towns. They wanted to take the tribe's land for farming and mining.

The Muscogee disagreed on how to save their lands. Some wanted to give up their traditions to live peacefully with white Americans. Others wanted to fight white settlers to protect their ancestors' way of life. Fighting broke out in 1813. The U.S. government sent General Andrew Jackson to take on the Muscogee who were against the white settlers.

*A battle took place at Fort Mims, Alabama, in 1813 between white settlers and the Creek.*

*Muscogee Chief Red Eagle met with General Andrew Jackson in 1815 to try to make peace.*

Now the Muscogee faced huge troubles. Their greatest treasure—their homelands—began to slip away. In 1814 the U.S. government took away a majority of Muscogee lands in both Georgia and Alabama. Earlier, in 1790, some Muscogee leaders from Georgia had sold lands to the U.S. government without permission from the tribe's government.

Tragedy lay ahead for the tribe. Andrew Jackson, who had been elected president, convinced Congress to pass the Indian Removal Act in 1830. It forced the Muscogee and four other southeastern tribes off their lands.

**tradition:** custom, idea, or belief passed down through time

# TRAIL OF TEARS

Between 1831 and 1838, U.S. soldiers forced more than 100,000 American Indians of various tribes out of their homelands. About 21,000 Muscogee men, women, and children left their homes and moved to unsettled territory in the West. More than 3,000 Muscogee and other Indians died along this journey that became known as the Trail of Tears.

The U.S. government considered some Muscogee to be allies. They were able to stay and remain on their land in Alabama. But most of the Muscogee rebuilt their lives along the Arkansas and Canadian rivers in present-day Oklahoma. They built homes and farmed. Leaders from each town continued to meet as a council to make decisions for the tribe.

Peaceful life did not last. The American Civil War nearly tore the Muscogee tribe apart in the 1860s. Tribe members fought on both sides and faced each other in bloody battles. American armies destroyed Muscogee homes, fields, and cattle. After the war ended in 1865, the U.S. government took half of Muscogee territory.

*Creek from 34 tribes gathered in front of the Creek Council House in the late 1800s in present-day Oklahoma.*

## Special ashes

On the Trail of Tears, the Muscogee carried ashes from the sacred fires in their eastern villages. They spread the ashes at the base of a great oak tree in present-day Tulsa, Oklahoma.

The tribe began to put itself back together in 1867. The Muscogee wrote a constitution and called itself the Muscogee Creek Nation. A principal chief, a group of judges, and lawmakers would lead the new government. They built a Council House in the new capital in Okmulgee, in present-day Oklahoma.

New troubles soon threatened to destroy the Muscogee Creek Nation. The U.S. Congress passed the Dawes Act in 1887 and the Curtis Act in 1898. The laws did not allow the Muscogee Nation to have its own government. They divided up the beloved lands the tribe shared. Tribe members received small, separate plots.

The Muscogee struggled to hold on to their nation. Even through this difficult time, a principal chief continued to lead them. For decades tribal leaders demanded their land and government back. By 1968 the U.S. government returned most territories in Oklahoma.

## FINDING ANCESTORS ONLINE

The U.S. government collected the names of members of five Oklahoma tribes from 1898 to 1907. Tribe members on the list, called the Dawes Rolls, could receive a piece of land when tribal lands were divided.

Today the lists are online. People can search for Muscogee ancestors through the Oklahoma Historical Society's website. Staff members at the Muscogee Creek Nation's collection of historical records can also identify ancestors. Finding ancestors' names on the Dawes Rolls can help people learn about their family history. With information about Muscogee ancestors, they can apply to become *citizens* of the Muscogee Creek Nation.

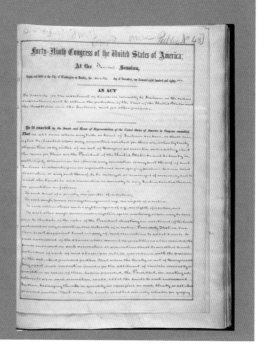

**constitution:** legal document that describes the basic form of the government and the rights of citizens

**citizen:** member of a country or state who has the right to live there

# Chapter 3

# Muscogee Life Today

Almost 80,000 Muscogee people are citizens of a federally recognized tribe. The Muscogee Creek Nation is located in Oklahoma. A second Muscogee tribe is in Alabama. There more than 3,000 members belong to the Poarch Band of Creeks. Muscogee citizens are also U.S. citizens.

Muscogee government today mixes new ideas with traditional ideas. The tribe elects a principal chief to four-year terms, similar to U.S. presidents. They elect members to a group similar to their ancestors' tribal council. The National Council makes laws for the nation. Judges and courts form the judicial branch of government. The tribes also have their own police forces and hospitals.

## Oklahoma nations

A U.S. stamp printed in 1948 lists the five tribes of the Intertribal Council—the Cherokee, Chickasaw, Choctaw, Muscogee, and Seminole.

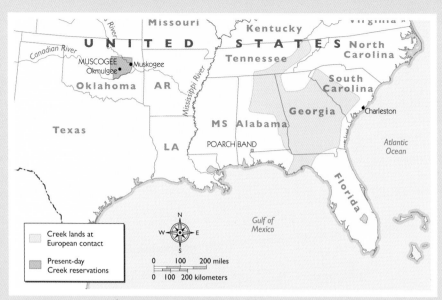

*Muscogee Creek Nation reservations are located in two states.*

The Muscogee still believe that uniting tribes makes them stronger. Muscogee **representatives** attend the Intertribal Council. They join representatives from four other nations—the Cherokee, Chickasaw, Choctaw, and Seminole. All five tribes were moved west during the Trail of Tears. Together they discuss topics affecting them all today.

The Muscogee Creek Nation shares news through its newspaper, television and radio stations, and texts to tribe members' phones. But new technology does not make the tribe forget its history—it connects the tribe just as rivers connected their ancestors' villages.

**representative:** someone who is chosen to act or speak for others

# WORK

The Muscogee tribe has never stopped farming. Today they operate large farms with modern equipment and plant soybeans and wheat. Some farmers share the harvest with their community as their ancestors did.

Tourists often visit the Muscogee Creek Nation. Tourism creates jobs for tribe members. Muscogee people work on golf courses and in restaurants, hotels, and shops. They also help run museums and historic sites.

The Muscogee Creek Nation government looks after its businesses. It gives advice and money to help them grow and hire more people. The nation trains tribe members for jobs in nursing and computer technology. The Muscogee Creek Nation shares the **profits** of its businesses with the community. The money flows to schools and to programs that care for elders in their nation.

A Creek man demonstrates traditional tools for tourists.

Each year as many as 20,000 Muscogee people gather for the Ocmulgee Indian Celebration in Macon, Georgia. The event takes place at Ocmulgee National Monument. Muscogee tribe members travel east to stand on the same ground as their ancestors. They can visit the flat-topped mounds of earth built by their ancestors' hands. The mounds were once used for ceremonies, burial grounds, and as defensive protection from enemies.

Visitors from outside the tribe join tribe members in celebrating Muscogee traditions. They listen to stories and cane flute music.

They watch demonstrations of stomp dances and stickball games. They experiment with making clay pottery and visit a traditional house built with plaster and river cane.

The mounds at Ocmulgee National Monument in Macon, Georgia, were built more than 1,000 years ago.

## SEEDS OF HISTORY

The Muscogee Creek Nation collects seeds passed down by their ancestors. The seeds are dried and stored at a cool temperature in what's known as a seed bank. Muscogee want their children to plant traditional foods to remember their history.

**profit:** money that a business makes after expenses have been subtracted

# Chapter 4

# Connecting to the Past

In the mid-1800s, Muscogee parents disagreed on how to prepare their children for the future. Some invited white Americans to teach their children to read and write in English. Others wanted their children to only learn about Muscogee culture. Beginning in the 1880s, the U.S. government forced Muscogee children to attend **boarding schools**. Along with children of other tribes, they had to leave their families. They had to cut their long hair and dress like white Americans.

*Muscogee children were taken from their homes and forced to attend boarding schools.*

Today Muscogee believe schools are tools for protecting their traditions. Almost all Muscogee children attend public schools in Oklahoma or Alabama. But Muscogee families help educate their children like their ancestors did. Parents work closely with teachers and school leaders to supervise programs for their children.

The U.S. government also helps Muscogee students remember their traditions. Government programs give money to schools for training teachers working with Muscogee students. The money also pays for Muscogee storytellers, dancers, and musicians to teach students about their traditions.

Young tribe members learn about their history at college. The Muscogee Creek Nation helps them pay for their studies. They can learn about tribal history at the College of the Muscogee Nation in Okmulgee and at some other Oklahoma colleges.

## PROTECTING MVSKOKE

Tribes in the Muscogee Confederacy spoke different languages. But speaking Mvskoke with each other united them. Today Muscogee leaders believe that only one in 10 tribe members can speak Mvskoke well.

The Muscogee nearly lost their language in the 1800s. Muscogee children were punished for speaking Mvskoke in boarding schools. But in schools today, children translate English into Mvskoke in front of judges. They compete for medallions and plaques.

The tribe works to make sure members do not forget their ancestors' language. Young people attend summer camps where they are encouraged to speak Mvskoke as much as possible. The Muscogee Creek Nation also has programs that train people to teach adults the language. Online programs allow tribe members to learn the language from home.

**boarding school:** school where students live away from home

## HOMES

The Muscogee make sure all tribe members have shelter. The tribal council lends money to tribe members to buy homes inside the nation. The government has housing assistance available for tribe members to rent homes at low prices. The Muscogee Creek Nation has programs that help elderly tribe members take care of their homes and yards at no charge.

Building communal spaces is also important to the Muscogee. Their ancestors gathered for ceremonies in circular buildings that could hold up to 500 people. Today up to 2,000 people can gather inside the Mvskoke Dome in Okmulgee, Oklahoma, for conferences, festivals, and sporting events.

*A 1565 drawing of a Creek village features a meeting house in the center surrounded by dwellings.*

## FOOD

The Muscogee still look after all their tribe members. The Muscogee Creek Nation wants no tribe member to go hungry. Tribe members in need can pick up donated food at the nation's warehouses and grocery stores. Every month the nation delivers thousands of meals to homes of the tribe's elders. It organizes classes on healthy eating habits for all tribe members.

The Muscogee want young people to enjoy the taste of their ancestors' food. At cooking classes elders teach tribe members to make a traditional dish called *vce taklike*

*The sour batter mixture for sour cornbread ages two to four days before it is baked in the oven.*

*kvmokse*, known as sour cornbread. Young people also learn to make blue corn bread dyed with purple hull peas and grape dumplings made from flour, sugar, and grape juice.

*Ancestors of today's Muscogee played stickball, and the tradition continues.*

## SPORTS

Teams of Muscogee race across fields for games of stickball. Armed with sticks topped with baskets, they scoop up a small ball and try to hit the top of a tall pole. Their ancestors played the game to train for war and to honor their gods. Today tribe members play after all-night stomp dances.

Tribe members take over fields to play softball. But they also roll a polished stone disk to play the ancient game of *chunkey*. Crowds at festivals cheer as two players run, trying to hit the target with long spears.

## BELIEFS

Muscogee today mix traditional and new beliefs. But in the 1800s, some tribe members feared the tribe would forget traditional beliefs. They even punished tribe members for practicing Christianity. Christian churches eventually became important meeting places for the tribe. Today most Muscogee are Baptist or Methodist. They sing Christian songs in the Muscogee language.

Tribe members also gather in special open areas called ceremonial grounds to honor traditional beliefs. They shuffle rhythmically around a fire. Men sing while women shake turtle shell rattles tied to their legs. Tribe members teach each other stomp dances at community centers.

### Health and wellness

Muscogee tribe members go to doctors when they are ill. The Muscogee Creek Nation owns a large, modern hospital. But tribe members might also visit traditional healers. The healers use wild plants and music to chase away spirits they believe cause illness.

## CELEBRATING TRADITIONS

In the month of June, the Muscogee gather to celebrate their traditions at the Mvskoke Nation Festival in Okmulgee, Oklahoma. Visitors from outside the tribe also come to have fun and to learn. They can join in a large stomp dance circling a fire.

Muscogee women wear colorful dresses stitched with ribbons like their ancestors wore to dance. Men wear boots and jeans with shirts decorated with ribbon. For dances men wear porcupine hair headdresses.

Crowds cluster around tables serving hamburgers but also traditional grape dumplings and pumpkin slices fried and dipped in sugar. Muscogee artisans display handmade traditional crafts—cane flutes, beaded jewelry, and woven belts and blankets. While members of the Muscogee Creek Nation celebrate with old and new friends, they never forget to look back at their ancestors' way of life as they move toward the future.

# TIMELINE

**1540s:** Spanish explorer Hernando de Soto crossed Muscogee lands looking for gold.

**1670s:** British, French, and Spanish begin to set up trading posts and settlements near Muscogee territory.

**1790:** Muscogee in Georgia sell tribal land to the United States.

**1813–1814:** The Muscogee fight a civil war. General Andrew Jackson ends the fighting.

**1836–1837:** The U.S. government forces more than 20,000 Muscogee to move to Indian Territory in present-day Oklahoma.

**1867:** The Muscogee write a new constitution. They name Okmulgee in present-day Oklahoma their capital.

**1887:** U.S. Congress passes the Dawes Act. It calls for Indian reservation lands to be divided among individuals but does not apply to the Muscogee.

**1898:** U.S. Congress passes the Curtis Act, which destroys the Muscogee government and allows Muscogee tribal lands to be broken up under the Dawes Act.

**1950:** Muscogee living in the East establish their nation near Poarch, Alabama.

**1970–1980:** Muscogee leaders write a new constitution, which is approved by tribal members. The tribe now calls itself the Muscogee Creek Nation.

**1980s:** The U.S. Supreme Court supports the right of Muscogee to tax its people and run its own court system.

**1984:** U.S. government recognizes the Poarch Band of Creek Indians.

**2004:** The College of the Muscogee Nation is established.

**2009:** President Barack Obama signs bill that includes text apologizing to American Indians for "many instances of violence, maltreatment, and neglect."

**2015:** The Muscogee Creek Nation National Council continues to meet on a monthly basis to discuss issues, such as health and welfare, land and natural resources, cultural preservation, and business and finance.

# GLOSSARY

**ally** (AL-eye)—person, group, or country that helps and supports another

**ancestor** (AN-sess-tur)—family member who lived a long time ago

**boarding school** (BOR-ding SKOOL)—school where students live away from home

**citizen** (SI-tuh-zuhn)—member of a country or state who has the right to live there

**confederacy** (kuhn-FE-druh-see)—union of people or groups with a common goal

**constitution** (kahn-stuh-TOO-shuhn)—legal document that describes the basic form of the government and the rights of citizens

**council** (KOUN-suhl)—group of people elected to make decisions for a larger group

**descendant** (di-SEN-duhnt)—person who comes from a particular group of ancestors

**elder** (EL-dur)—older person whose experience makes him or her a leader

**profit** (PROF-it)—money that a business makes after expenses have been subtracted

**representative** (rep-ri-ZEN-tuh-tiv)—someone who is chosen to act or speak for others

**sacred** (SAY-krid)—holy

**tradition** (truh-DISH-uhn)—custom, idea, or belief passed down through time

# READ MORE

**Schwartz, Heather E.** *Forced Removal: Causes and Effects of the Trail of Tears.* Cause and Effect: American Indian History. North Mankato, Minn.: Capstone Press, 2015.

**Stone, Amy M.** *Creek History and Culture.* Native American Library. New York: Gareth Stevens Pub., 2012.

**Waterby, Ralph.** *Muscogee (Creek).* Spotlight on Native Americans. New York: PowerKids Press, 2016.

# INTERNET SITES

FactHound offers a safe, fun way to find Internet sites related to this book. All of the sites on FactHound have been researched by our staff.

Here's all you do:

Visit *www.facthound.com*

Type in this code: 9781515702382

Check out projects, games and lots more at
**www.capstonekids.com**

# CRITICAL THINKING USING THE COMMON CORE

1. Early Muscogee believed in communal property, not private property. How do Muscogee today share property among their citizens? (Key Ideas and Details)

2. How did the Muscogee alliance with Great Britain influence Muscogee history? How did things change for the Muscogee after the United States won its independence from Great Britain? (Integration of Knowledge and Ideas)

3. In what ways do Muscogee parents help their children remember their ancestors? (Key Ideas and Details)

# INDEX